Manna in the Morning

Manna in the Morning

Poems by

Jacqueline Jules

Cover design by Shay Culligan
Cover image by Giorgio Parravicini via unsplash.com
Author photograph by Alan Hechtkopf

ISBN: 978-1-954353-01-5

Kelsay Books
502 South 1040 East, A-119
American Fork, Utah, 84003

For my Mussar group at Temple Rodef Shalom, Virginia

Acknowledgments

The author would like to thank the following publications where the poems listed below first appeared, some in earlier versions with different titles.

Bourgeon: "Jochebed"
Dove Tales: "Patience"
Hedge Apple: "Trees of the Talmud"
Jewish Women's Literary Annual: "Facing the Wilderness,"
    "Ner Tamid"
The Literary Nest: "Narrow Bridge"
Lowestoft Chronicle: "Lot's Wife"
Mizmor Anthology: "Building a Tabernacle," "Jonah and Noah,"
    "Invoking Shechinah"
The New Verse News: "On the Altar"
Poetica: "Birth Order," "The Glory of the Journey," "Miracles
    in the Desert," "Yom Kippur Offering"
A Poet's Siddur: "Dialogue with the Divine," "Manna in
    the Morning," "We Want to Know Why"
Shirim: A Jewish Poetry Journal: "Prenuptials," "Wrestling"
Spirit First: "Mirrored Light," "To Be a Gold Droplet Floating"
Voice of Eve: "Questioning Eve"
What Rough Beast: "The City of Sodom," "Practicing Humility"
YARN Magazine: "The Consolation of Clouds"

Contents

Biblical Lives

Jacob stole his brother's birthright.
Moses murdered an Egyptian.
David seduced another man's wife.

The Bible elevates lives
marked by more than merit.

Yet unlike Twitter, the Bible
doesn't cancel characters. We are told
to read beyond the transgression,
consider the whole saga.

To remember the Israelites
were not abandoned
after the Golden Calf.

And each one of us
is Abraham and Sarah,
Isaac and Rebecca—
more complex
than our worst moments
or our best.

Truth

In Spanish,
the word is "verdad."
The French call it "vérité."
Germans use "wahrheit."
So on and so forth.

Every culture has its own term
for what should be
just as obvious to you as to me.

Yet even when we share
language, we differ
in dialects, making it hard
to hear anyone unlike ourselves.

If you believe the Bible,
the Tower of Babel is to blame.

That time, when we were so anxious
to reach the place where power resides,
we lost the ability to speak to each other.

Questioning Eve

How did Eve adjust
after leaving Eden?

Did she absorb
the pain of childbirth
as a reasonable price
for sweet bliss
suckling her breast?

Or did she spend
the rest of her days
missing the limits of Eden
where as long as she didn't eat
from the Tree of Knowledge,
she would not be touched
by hunger of any kind?

Prenuptials

Vows exchanged. Papers signed.
Will they bind me back to Adam's rib?
To move from that day on
in synchrony, for fear
of ripping apart the flesh we share.

Eve was a bulge beneath the armpit
whittled when the first wife, Lilith,
ran away. Must I leave the garden,
become a demon,
to preserve the person
who precedes the wedding?

Maybe not. Our book has been revised.
But the snake still lurks in the garden
and we must choose our fruit with care.

Abraham's Youth

Is it possible Abraham
was never a convert?

He never bowed down
like others in his city
to statues of silver and gold.
Even as a child, he understood
idols had eyes but do not see;
ears, but do not hear.

Does it make the story better?

To see Abraham holy from birth,
always fit to sire three nations,
as numerous as the stars in the sky.

A man never swayed
by community custom,
never guilty of a heathen remark,
unearthed decades later to prove
he once worshipped idols.

Is purity truly more plausible
than a convert with the courage
to cast off his father's vile ways
and heed the call for change?

The City of Sodom

Abraham was not Noah,
content to save his family
while everyone else drowned.

Abraham argued for Sodom.

Is this justice from the Judge
of the world, that the righteous
be dealt the same blow as the guilty?

Abraham bargained.

Will you save Sodom
for 50 innocent lives?

What about 45?

40? 30? 20? 15?

In the end, they settled.

Ten decent souls
could save an entire city.

And Sodom was lacking even that.

A fact to remember
the next time I question
if the compassion
of one person counts.

Lot's Wife

The pavement abruptly ended
at two dirt roads
winding off beneath blue skies,
dotted with feathery clouds
in question mark shapes.

Both choices too narrow
with too many ruts and stones.
Yet one had a trace more sunlight
swirling in the dust.

Closing my eyes, I hit the gas,
thinking of Lot's wife,
and how she turned into
a pillar of salt
when she looked back.

Of All the Drama

Sarah is famous for her laugh,
the one that questioned
if a withered old woman
could produce a child.

And she's blamed
for the banishment of Hagar,
cruel treatment of a rival.

Yet we don't discuss that business
in Egypt too much, when her husband
acknowledged her beauty and fretted
for his own safety, not hers.

"Say you are my sister,"
Abraham pleaded. "Not my wife."

Thus, Sarah was seized
for Pharaoh's palace while Abraham
acquired oxen and sheep.

In time, she was released
to travel again with the husband
who put his needs above hers.

Of all the drama in the Bible,
for me, this rings the most true—
a woman who forgives a man
to continue their historic journey.

Jonah and Noah

In the last hours of Yom Kippur,
as I sit with a rumbling stomach,
reflecting on regrets, I read
the story of Jonah, that prophet
who ran away when asked
to save a city, who refused
Divine request.

How does he compare?
To the story Jews read
a few weeks later
about Noah, a man who
never questioned God, who
simply picked up a hammer
to do as he was told.

Two men from the Torah
with rhyming names.

One said, "yes."
The other, "no."

Jonah didn't want to try.
Noah didn't see a choice.

Who will I be
as this stormy year unfolds?

The one who sits in the belly of a whale,
clutching anger, frustration, and fear?

Or the one who finds wood and builds a ship
to survive the oncoming flood?

Looking Beyond

Floating, after the flood,
Noah stood on the ark
searching the horizon
for a mountaintop,
a safe space
above the water.

He sent out a dove,
willing to believe,
even after forty days
and forty nights of rain,
trees could still exist.

The dove brought back
an olive branch.

Proof that if you look
beyond flood waters,
there will be dry land.

Mirrored Light

The moon's light
is only an illusion,
a reflection of the sun,
shining beyond sight.

Yet each month,
I watch a slim crescent
wax to a brilliant orb
and consider
how luminous
my life would be,
if I could mirror light
from the heavens
like that.

Wrestling

Turning, Jacob sensed the stranger
crouching in the darkness.
Alone, with no one to witness cowardice
or courage, he fought all night,
emerging at daybreak, intact,
save for a hip wrenched from its socket.

Last night, my sobs
scorched the ceiling
as I wrestled a stranger, too.
But who pummeled me?
An angel?
Or my own embodied anger?
We rolled over and over
punching each other's faces,
neither gaining dominance until dawn
when my assailant blessed my struggle
and dissolved into a shining light.

My thigh throbs as I limp away.

Waiting by the Side of the Road

Rachel is weeping for her children.
  —Jeremiah 31:15

Dying in childbirth, Rachel was buried
by the side of the road, an odd fate
for a beloved wife, never really explained
except to say her resting place
meant she could see her children passing by
and weep for them, pray for their safety.

Thousands visit Rachel's tomb each year,
believing her love can travel through time.

While I know my grave will not inspire
pilgrimage or be deserving of the dome
Rachel rests beneath, it would console me
to think I could wait by the side of the road,
watching for those I love, always ready
to offer a mother's embrace.

Esau's Choice

We know Jacob's fears, watching
his brother Esau approach
flanked by four hundred men.

The text describes the terror
of a man who swindled a birthright
and stole a blessing, who realized
revenge might be justified.

But what about Esau,
the brother Jacob wronged?

Did he march with his hand
on his hip, gripping his sword
until the moment he saw Jacob
prostrate on the ground?

Did the gifts Jacob offered really matter?

The Bible reveals no details, no reason
why Esau kissed his brother and wept.

We can only imagine why no blood
was shed, no rage reenacted.

And hope that Esau's choice
will be the one we choose
in our homes, too.

Patience

The patient person shows much good sense, but the quick-tempered one displays folly at its height.

—Proverbs 14:29

It's a heavy box

I can't drop
without
smashing
my toe.

A prompt.

Reminding me
to set the package down
before speaking.

To consider what will burn
before I strike a match.

To take advantage
of the split second
before the flicker lights the fuse
when the flame could sputter,
and the hot anger between us
could fade to warmth.

Birth Order

With my feet in the stirrups
and the baby's head crowning,
it's too late to say,
Next on the list. Not now.

Yet, every morning,
I grunt and push,
birthing tasks I fret
should be finished in a different order.
Gym first? Or thesis?
Groceries? Or garbage?
Will meeting A be better than meeting B?
Should I floss now or later?

True, the firstborn inherits more.
But even twins emerge one at a time,
no matter how much they fight in the womb.

It did Jacob little good to hold Esau's heel.
The blessing still had to be stolen.
He still had to flee Canaan.
And Rebecca's bid to direct destiny
drove away both her sons.

Wondering about Dinah and Leah

Bible stories are skeletal, bones
fleshed out through exegesis—
words, sentences, translations
scrutinized, interpreted.

And most dwell on the men,
on actions, not emotions.

In Genesis 34, we don't hear from Dinah
herself, only what was done to her.
And we hear nothing from Leah,
her mother, who should have been waiting,
worrying, ready to comfort.

Did Dinah find solace with Leah?
The woman remembered
as the unloved wife, the one forced on
Jacob instead of the sister he favored.

I wonder as I read the exploits of men,
the brothers who claimed
defense of a sister's honor
required mass murder and pillage.

And I wonder if Dinah and Leah ever discussed
what happened. Or if Dinah had to accept,
as I did, that a jealous woman, disappointed
in her own life, lacks the skills
to console a daughter.

The Consolation of Clouds

In its gaseous state,
water is colorless and odorless,
so imperceptible,
it could be called imaginary.

But when this same
colorless vapor condenses
miles above the ground
majestic white mountains
appear in a blue diamond sky.

And the sunlight
streaming through
serrated shapes
feels like fingers
reaching down
to wipe the tears
from my cheeks.

Joseph's Fortune and Mine

If not for jealous brothers
and a convenient pit, Joseph would
have stayed in Canaan, favored by Jacob,
flaunting his multicolored coat.

But no worries, he found success as a slave
in Egypt. Appointed head of household
until Potiphar's wife brazenly pursued
his beautiful biceps.

Behind bars for a crime he didn't commit,
Joseph foretold dreams, serenely waiting
for favor to find him again in Pharaoh's court.

So if not for the pit, Potiphar's wife, and prison
Joseph would not have been dressed in royal robes
welcoming his brothers with generous guile.

Good fortune following calamity. A phenomenon
enjoyed by more than Joseph in Genesis—
if I stop sniffling long enough to note where
each crooked turn in the road has ended for me.

If only I'd cried less when cast aside in a pit,
felt less jilted by a jealous world plotting against me.
Maybe like Joseph, I too would have waited
with fewer complaints for a better destiny to unfold.

Jochebed

Baby Moses floated
down the Nile,
in a basket caulked
with bitumen and pitch,
carefully constructed
from a mother's
calculated choice
to set her child adrift
amid crocodiles
rather than see him slain
before her eyes.

I think of Jochebed today
as I set you down among tall reeds
knowing you will float
to a fate beyond my grasp
in a wicker basket
I can't make watertight.

But clamping you against my breast
will not keep soldiers or crocodiles away.

So I stand aside, praying for a princess
to scoop you from the water with a kiss.

Crossing the Red Sea

The rabbis say
Reuven and Shimon
crossed the Red Sea,
eyes down, grumbling,
so engrossed in grievances
they missed the miracle
of the waters parting.

Fleeing affliction,
I've been guilty, too,
of seeing only
the mud beneath my feet,
dwelling on the bricks
and burdened backs of Egypt,
ignoring outstretched arms
ready to hold me until
I reach the other side.

Dialogue with the Divine

When I petition,
I'm on my knees, bruised
by the hardness of the floor.

I'm an Israelite,
obsessed by the squish
of mud under my sandals,
ignoring the Red Sea,
miraculously parted.

When I praise,
I'm on my feet, billowing
like clouds in a sapphire sky.

I'm Miriam
holding a tambourine,
dancing in the desert, grateful
for the smallest excuse
to sing.

To Be a Gold Droplet Floating

While sometimes
prayer dissolves me
like sugar in water
to become
a sweeter substance,
I am just as satisfied
with suspension
in this oil and vinegar world.

To be a gold droplet floating
in a dark, mysterious sea
certain
I can withstand
a hard shaking
and not be absorbed
by bitter circumstances.

Facing the Wilderness

Twelve scouts went into Canaan.
Ten saw giants too big to fight
while two saw grapes too big to carry.

"We are like grasshoppers in the land,"
the ten cried, "sure to be crushed."

"Not true," Joshua and Caleb argued.

Steadfast, they predicted victory
while the rest shrieked and mourned
imagined defeat.

In the end, only the two survived
to reach their destination.

An instructive tale for me
as I consider the faith needed
to see grapes instead of giants
in the wilderness waiting ahead.

Manna in the Morning

Cook fires,
clothing scraps,
animal dung
have long disappeared
from the desert.
But the story remains:
how the Israelites
fled Pharaoh
under a spiral
of swirling white clouds
as angels swept
stones and snakes
from their path.

For forty years,
Jews followed Moses
with manna-filled bellies,
thirst quenched by
a wondrous wandering well—
the same fountain I sipped
this candlelit evening
with honeyed challah
and roasted chicken.

Carrying dishes to the sink,
my sandaled feet skip
on a freshly swept floor,
free of snakes and stones.

Tonight, Pharaoh lies drowned
behind me
and I am traveling to Canaan
under a sheltering white cloud,
certain of manna in the morning.

Miracles in the Desert

Like the favorite dish
a parent cooks all afternoon
to please a child,
manna was a special treat
on each tongue. To some,
it tasted like bread. For others,
it was honey. Gathered by hand
from the desert, it became
whatever was desired
in the exact portion needed.

No one had too much or too little.

And like a parent animating
bedtime stories, the voice at Sinai
mirrored the manna, ringing
from the mountain in tones
tempered for each waiting ear.
Some leaned forward for a whisper
while others stepped back from a roar.
No two accounts concurred,
but not one soul doubted another.

Miracles, we study over and over,
longing to see once more.

The Glory of the Journey

Forty years Moses
wandered in the desert
to reach a land
he would never walk upon.

With awe,
we laud and remember
the majestic figure
standing on Mount Nebo,
gazing at his dream.

Someone else led
the Israelites into Canaan,
waged successful battles
and enjoyed final victory
amid the milk and honey.

Not Moses,
whose greatness is measured
by the glory of his journey,
undiminished
by a destination
never reached.

We Want to Know Why

Like the animals in Noah's ark
Everything walks by its mate.
There is no Light without Dark.
No Large without Small.

A front and a back to everything.
Hard, Soft. Hot, Cold. Healthy, Sick.

Still, we want to know why

Up is defined by Down.

Joy sits on a seesaw with Grief.

We are Moses on the mountain
begging to behold a Presence,
allowed only a glimpse
as we cower in the cleft of a rock.

Humbled, we climb down,
stone tablets clutched to our chest,
lay them tenderly in the tabernacle
to carry on weary shoulders,
through years in the wilderness,
always pining for the Divine Face
we won't be permitted to see.

Building a Tabernacle

And let them make me a sanctuary so that I may dwell among them.
—Exodus 25:8

Human hands, not divine,
gathered acacia wood
and precious metal.

The Jews were generous,
offering their own linen
and gold, stones and silver.

No one questioned why
the tabernacle did not
appear as a gift like manna.

No one expected the work
to be completed for them.

Inspiration for me
as I struggle to build
a space inside my heart
where holiness can dwell.

The Tabernacle of #MeToo

When the Israelites built an ark
for the holy tablets,
they chose acacia wood
and lined it with gold—
that strong gleaming element
only corroded by greed.

Yet once the ark was finished,
not even the priests
were privileged to peek inside.

Why did they use precious metal
for an interior no one sees?

Ancient logic lost
on powerful men today
who feel no pressure
to present
the same golden face
in private as in public.

Practicing Humility

No more than my space, no less than my place.
—Alan Morinis, *Every Day, Holy Day*

All have a seat in the sanctuary.
One space. No more, no less.

How do I fill mine?

Sitting so still, hands in my lap,
no one feels my presence?

Or stretching long limbs,
elbowing, kicking others?

I have a seat in the sanctuary,
to lift my book and sing my hymn,
just as you have a seat beside me.

One space. No more, no less.

A Rare Soul

David hid in a field,
watching Jonathan raise his bow,
trusting the son of King Saul
to shoot arrows as a signal to flee.

Why?

By then, Jonathan should have
seen David as a rival.
Should have considered
using the weapon in his hand
to please his father
and secure the throne
he lost by saving David's life.

Instead, Jonathan remained the friend
who honored David with his own
cloak and tunic, literally
offering the shirt off his back.

Maybe Jonathan was impressed,
like everyone else, by the boy
who slew the giant Goliath
with a simple slingshot.

Or maybe he was just a rare soul, unlike
the rest of us, happy to be remembered
as the most loyal of friends,
instead of a powerful king.

Wherever You Go, I Will Go

Seeing the words alone,
you might think they were spoken
by a woman sacrificing her needs
to follow a man. Instead, Ruth's pledge
to Naomi proclaimed a bond
between two women, navigating
a world where widows
survived on leftover grain
and the kindness of kinsman.

Much is made of Ruth's marriage
to Boaz, how a faithful convert
declared *your people will be my people,*
and became the great-grandmother
of David, the king, line of the Messiah.

May we not forget how the story began,
with two homeless, grief-stricken women,
supporting each other through hard times.

Hannah's Heart

Before Hannah wept
in the sanctuary at Shiloh,
we didn't believe it possible
to beseech the One above
without blood.
We burned bulls to please.
Men measured portions.
More for the fertile wife.
Less for the barren one.

Before Hannah wept,
prayer was public,
not a plea from within
by a woman who taught us
to move our lips in silence,
pouring out pain so personal
I can hear Hannah's heart
within me tonight.

She tells me my anguish is holy
and if I articulate sorrow
I may find the strength
to rise from my knees
and go forth in peace
the way she did.

Ner Tamid

Not the usual red plastic bulb
safely suspended
on a chain above the ark,
but a gas flame, breathing light.

My body sits
as decorum requests
but my eyes want to stand
in front of the sanctuary
and stare
at the shimmer
of flaming fingers
shadowed on the ceiling.

Did Moses feel this way,
watching a bush burn
without destruction?

Like Hannah, my lips move
in soundless prayer. The flame
listens, lifting shadows
with each supplication.

This is not a general promise
for generations
beyond Mount Sinai.

This covenant is personal,
bestowed in a house
where a living flame
burns above the Torah,
kindling faith in a heart
inflamed by grief.

Narrow Bridge

The world is a narrow bridge and the most important thing is not to be afraid.

—Rebbe Nachman of Breslov

I stand on a narrow bridge,
the width of a whisper,
connecting today to tomorrow.

The abyss breathes below,
ready to swallow my screams.

Once, I trusted
in a tender Presence
steadying my elbow,
providing a rail.

Now, I am tempted to look down.

To question the choice to cross at all.

But the most important thing,
I am told,
is not to fear.

Keep moving.
On tiptoe, if need be.

Stop waiting
for something to hold.

Western Wall Meditation

From the beginning,
we have sought the safety of walls
to shield us
from animals, enemies, the elements.

Within their sheltering presence,
we dine and rest,
raise babies and grow old.

Giving thanks,
we erect more walls
and gather to worship.

Walls embrace our songs,
listen to our praise,
accept our petitions.

But even strong structures crumble,
leaving one-fourth of what was.

Then memory supports us,
enclosing our faith
as we weep and pray.

Queen Esther

"If I perish, I perish,"
the young queen tells the mirror.
Donning jewels and perfume,
she strides in silk gown toward her fate.

"If I perish, I perish."
Is it really courage that lifts her chin?
A noble choice to swing from the gallows
rather than hide in silence?

"If I perish, I perish."
Or does action offer its own rewards
when you're likely to hang
by the neck either way?

The Trees of the Talmud

*If you have a sapling in your hand and someone tells you the
Messiah has arrived, first plant the sapling and then go out
to welcome the Messiah.*

—Rabbi Yochanan ben Zakkai

Talmud sages
cite the old man
cheerfully planting
a carob tree, unbothered
by the seventy year wait
for the chewy pods
fondly recalled from youth.

Never mind that a carob tree
yields in seven years, not seventy—
the Talmud and the Torah
don't offer logical numbers.

Only advice to plant first
and welcome the Messiah later.

To put every sapling in the ground
without counting how many years
before you or your children taste fruit.

You Shall Be Holy

You shall be holy to me, for I the Lord am holy.
—Leviticus 20:26

"Shall" to be understood
as command, not suggestion.

Visualizing a world
where no one profits
from the blood of another.

Where we see holiness
in the mirror and each other.

Where we are devoted
to deeds, not idols.

"Shall" to be understood
as command, not suggestion.

Yom Kippur Offering

Between the last sip of water
and the first bite of food,
twenty-four hours later,
there are words.

Pages and pages of words.
Spoken, chanted, mumbled, mouthed
in Hebrew and in English.

Words. Swirling in the fragile space
between faith and fear
like smoke from the burnt animal
our ancestors sacrificed.

Words. Offered with parched lips,
grumbling bellies,
and a fist against the heart.

We are arrogant,
slow to admit mistakes,
quick to accuse others,
unwilling to accept
that all deeds matter.

Words. Pierce concrete hearts
like the mythical shamir,
who cut stone
for Solomon's Temple.

Words. Waiting
for souls to emerge
chiseled and clean.

Invoking Shechinah

Visualize a silver light,
stroking your shoulders,
kissing your eyelids,
softly swirling
behind your neck

All around you

Shechinah

Shimmering, pulsing,
beating like wings

Imagine angels

Four of them

Michael on your right side,
arm holding your waist

Gabriel on your left side
whispering, "You can."

Uriel in front
finger pointing at the path

Raphael in back,
chanting the prayer of Moses
pleading for his sister Miriam,
"Please heal her. Heal her now."

On the Altar

*More than 140 children were sacrificed at about the same time
in Peru's northern coastal region, about 550 years ago.*
—BBC News, April 28, 2018

Remains of children and llamas in Peru
remind me of Abraham, how he didn't argue
for Isaac the way he did for Sodom and Gomorrah,
how he acquiesced, traveling three days as commanded,
building an altar, binding his son. Imagine
Isaac's terrified eyes until an angel appeared
with new instructions.

Which brings me back to the bodies in Peru,
breastbones bent to extract 140 hearts
offered to appease an angry god, demanding
what's most precious as ultimate bribe.

Like a folktale reinvented around the globe,
sacrifice is not confined to geographic region.
From ancient times, somehow humans have believed
we have to kill to demonstrate devotion.

When the angel told Abraham to offer a ram instead,
it was more than a revelation, it was a weaning.
Spiritually, we were babies, still sucking
on our first source of sustenance.

Think of how we despaired later on,
when the Temple was destroyed and
we were told we couldn't burn animals
anymore. What can we put on the altar now?
We cried. How do we please now?

The answer still eludes us.

The Scripture of My Life

Embarrassing episodes, compiled in short narratives,
could fill a white Bible, embossed with blue letters.
Browse verses 1-20 for the list of personalities
tried out in my teens, like jeans in a dressing room,
discarding bell-bottoms for boot cut,
low-waisted for high-rise, size 6 for size 10,
only to find them all uncomfortable.

Subsequent verses record hours
of teach yourself guitar while watching TV;
journal entries on poems never finished;
hot tears over an early college rejection,
a cheerleader's comment on my prom dress,
the boyfriend who impregnated a classmate.

It's all there, including my silent mouth
when an English advisor offered salvation
for my Jewish soul, followed by months
of pouring out the story in tall red cups
at every campus party. Verse 25 tells
how I waitressed half-blind, too vain
to wear old glasses. Verse 40 of too few calls home
after Daddy's first heart attack. Don't read Verse 56,
where I spilled coffee at an interview, snapped
at my mother-in-law, backed a car into a fence.

Youth shouldn't be reread without wine
on a Saturday night. Still, I have faith
in the way one verse begot another
until my present good fortune
of standing on the mountain
with the tablets in my hands,
not sorry at all that my days of
dancing with the Golden Calf are gone.

About the Author

Jacqueline Jules is the author of three chapbooks, *Field Trip to the Museum* (Finishing Line Press), *Stronger Than Cleopatra* (ELJ Publications), and *Itzhak Perlman's Broken String,* winner of the 2016 Helen Kay Chapbook Prize from Evening Street Press. She is also the author of 45 books for young readers, including the Zapato Power series, the Sofia Martinez series, *The Hardest Word, Never Say A Mean Word Again,* and *Tag Your Dreams: Poems of Play and Persistence.* Her poetry has appeared in over 100 publications, including *The Paterson Literary Review, The Broome Review, Sow's Ear Poetry Review, Hospital Drive,* and *Imitation Fruit.* She lives in Arlington, Virginia.

Please visit her online here:

jacquelinejules.com

metaphoricaltruths.blogspot.com/

www.ingramcontent.com/pod-product-compliance
Lightning Source LLC
Chambersburg PA
CBHW071358090426
42738CB00012B/3160